N.F.G

(NO F**KS GIVEN)

JORDAN CAMBRIDGE

ARTWORK BY JAMES NOBLE

Content Warning

This book is purely for entertainment purposes, containing strong language and themes that some may find offensive or disturbing.

This book loosely references real places, events and experiences but is not in any way intended to be biographical.

This book is not suitable for anyone under the age of 18.

For all my friends, who have helped me
carry on each day through my own personal
hell, which I've learned to call:
"the work".

Table of Contents:

Pick your Vibe...

Hippodrome.

I hear the idiot chatter outdoors.
The city life is happening.

I hold a middle finger to all its achievements.

You don't win,
but
a life you didn't die from,
but grieved,
was worth living.

Every word now
holds back tears.
Going about life.
Walking a hurt corpse round
the racetrack slower, and slower.

A performance.
A duty to an audience.

When it's over,
a crying, black draped applause
drawn across a portrait next to a black box.

You're not even there to take a bow.

The sad irony of it all.
Beauty ends in tragedy,
always.

The thorns
on the rose remain.
The petals,
still with some colour,
willing, and strong,
but withered,
wilt.

Buds form like memories
Not yet had.
They can't help us right now.

Why so sad?

Why choose run the lap?

You could, sprint,
or jog, walk, crawl, sit.
You can run,
really run
for the thrill of it.

Don't trick yourself,
it's all downhill.
The finish ribbon is, there;
waiting like a patient lover.
Keep it at your horizon,
and really live
every sunset.

Coronation.

We die several times throughout our lives.

We finally notice our bodies,
but so many times
have stared into the mirror
with a different mind.

"The Incorrect" - the epithet that should be on every
gravestone.

And the mind that now
knows the word epithet,
throws the bones
of the old fool into the Tiber.

The white throne room,
usurped and occupied
by the wiser.

To learn, is to die.

To fall on the sword of your ignorance.
The one you once used,
to revitalise
the philosophy of:
"This, is me"

This is who I am now.
My calling.

My journey into the eternal.
Permanent, steady sailing out of my mouth into the
new world;

What I, will be remembered for.

But they, now exist
only in old photographs
when you had your hair that way.

You awkwardly acknowledge it's you
in that abstract impression,

But you ask yourself

"who was that?"

You are impatient
because you are
a placeholder,
an imposter.

Stolen body,
knowing that you will find
yourself out.

You are only
the you,
that you are now.

Happy Place.

I remember the little boardwalk jetty on the lake.
Looking across at the mountains of Albania.

I have never been,
but the border from Montenegro seemed invisible.
I couldn't tell which water
was which,
the ripples from stones, uninterrupted.

The field on the other side a rich gold.
The mountains were grey, dusted white caps.

The trees were tall dark brushes on the sky,
timeless
in the summer air that held you like a blanket.

The lake was mirror-still.

I took in that scene deep into the back of my
retinas,
right into my soul.
Filled my mind with it,
and right there, it took me in
and I dropped away.

I chased it down
with a deep, mindful breath.

I thank every asshole, for every time
I must stop, to remember that place.

Lavender to Cover the Stench of Humanity.

Our lavender pots
placed on the front lawn
the day before
had the soil taken.
Scraped holes either side.

They're stealing dirt.

People are the worst.

She says things are returning to normal,
in a voice burning with melodic optimism.
Through bright green trees
I see alcoholics in the park,
(it's ok if it's a warm weekend).

They thoughtlessly clambered over a fence with the
grace of potato sacks.

A gate
is two social distances away.

Blue plastic bags clink with bottles.
And I try not to think the worst
of things being normal.
But,
someone stole,

fucking
dirt.

2 weeks later,
they took the whole pot.

What rotten rooted brutes,
who must cause
so much trouble for
themselves.

What did they have stolen from
the bottom of their hearts?

A sucky life is enough for my revenge.
Fuck'em.

Fuck off.

Fuck off.

Just fuck off.

I don't owe you.

I don't owe them.

I don't owe me.

Fuck it.

Fuck all of that.

I don't own it.

I don't need it.

I don't want it.

Fuck the future.

Fuck the past.

Fuck everyone.

Fuck you in advance.
Fuck 10 seconds ago.

Fuck tomorrow.

I'm staying here.

Right here.

Leave me alone.

And with the hot air blown away
Comes breathing.

The animal inside,
tricked into revealing itself.

It's ridiculous ire.
Nobody has ever died
when one feels like this.

In facing death,
this would not cross your mind.

What are you protecting?
What are you investing so much life into
that you would spoil
right now dude?

The War.

The grey skies weep,
grieved for the battleground to happen.
Soaked skin tents as handkerchiefs.

We wait in solemn, nervous rest, clinging to the
weary warmth of our bodies, doing our best to
honour our remaining cloudy winter breaths.

Mud smears like paint beneath enemy feet and spears.
The horn blows.
Battle commences.

Shields for the calamity of failed leadership.
Un-ending ideals conjured by circles of men in
chambers: powerful in the minds of those who plough
the fields,
work the lines
and fight
until broken in their own wars of corporations.

This, a muddy blood red eruption of the turbulence
underneath the surface.

Clatter, cracks, and slicks;
swords, shields and rifles buffed like crashing
waves.
The squelch of flesh
and the damp earth it returns to.

We paid
and paid in death.
Exchanged with crimson steel receipts
and scratched armour plates; full of dents and cuts
like skin frozen in time.
Like some of us,
it will never mend
but can always be replaced.

Did they die for lack of skill?
Were they good because they met their fate?
Stern faced
in the crosshair.

Or victims of commanders
who do not understand war?
Who grasp at old tactics, batons, and medals, rattled
like toys filled with bones.

Shaking their appointed power until it breaks and
spills.
Until the skulls roll
like dice across a map, or screen
with pixel men made of lights.

Whose mess is it to clean?

The enemy?
The unforeseen?
The leaders in the field who will be investigated?

The men in the chambers will speak to the people, of
bold sacrifice, while the dead remain nameless.

The Diner.

I feel out of sorts.

The words don't come.

They wait outside
the café diner writing scene
in my mind,
and ponder why
they should visit a man
who fell into this.

He didn't study Keats,
And only has a C, A.S in English.

My throat croaks and rasps,
just a little to make me nervous.
My chest, jaw and mind stay clenched.
Regardless of how horizontal I am, I can't call it
rest.

I can hear the murmur of the words outside.

The ones that say I'm sick push to the front of the
line,
Quick to get their fix in
and head back.

They knock on the glass door and ask if I'm open -
voice distorted
like a man in a fish tank.
I ignore them.

I might put my feet up again.

The lights in my head flicker sparsely,
whilst bluebottles buzz and bash into each other
in either a dog fight,
or two lovers
preparing to fuck
in the aroma of decay.

The lights flash as they hit each other like sparks.
The mental violence is unnecessary.
I'm closed for today.

Dead.

My arm extends in view of my open eye

as I lie down on my bed,

and I'm dead now.

My fingers curl effortlessly

like a dried-up spider.

Like you see in the movies.

Face, lifeless, out of frame.

I am dead,

dead from this day.

I can rest
like they do.

I seep into the earth.

Nothing to worry about.

I can't sleep but I don't need to.

I just need to be dead.

Imagine if they still think like we do?

They don't.

At last,

they realised
it was a cosmic blink.

They don't care

and they would laugh at us.

Maybe they can.

I doubt they have ever tried.

They like it down there.

Fall.

Don't fucking try so hard.
Don't try at all.

Free fall,

I call it: one directional flying.

Never has there been so much purpose and
inertia potential,
from waiting in suspension
to jump into bed.

You'll find
you do stuff anyway.

That's not a short attention span.

It's all you need.

It's realising that now
is the time.

Just then, maybe not.

The next, who knows when.

But when you are ready,

in bed,
dressed,
sunshine, or
moonlight,
whatever.

When you go go go.

That
was the time.

No one blows the wind.

Birds don't always fly,
bees don't always sting.

Good things come
to those who wait,
and
those
who wait,
come to good things.

I think, who knows really?

Isa.

Early morning.

The black sky leaks lazily.

Cold, biting rain,

tapping hordes.

It's a good day for staying indoors.

But I journey against my nature.

My inner child cries,
held close to my chest.

In that moment, I hate them for it.

My key chain clipped at my side,
percussion to my steps.

Gripped lightly between my fingers.

Had it for years.

More reliable than some friends.

I feel the hardness

of stainless-steel links,

the cold of the air.

I take both into my veins and

I just don't care.

Frames.

I spend more hours now,
focused on nothing.

The events are just stories,

re-enactments of what happened
organically.

The frames are just pictures of a
fixed world.
(without balls)

All the pictures outside

can only be lived,
touched,

and witnessed.

I'm wasting time.

Chewing it up,

digesting it.

Investing nothing.

Doing nothing.
Getting everything.

OK/s.

I'd have done better in the days of letters
because there's more thought and reading
before it goes out,
instead of
just shouting feelings.

I've had no signal on my phone
for the last 20 miles.

It is not being away
that I'm afraid of;
alone, staying
with my thoughts...

I asked for a black coffee.

She said.

"Any sauce?"
It's this.

This,
is talking.

The coffee was awful.

Needed sauce.

Nose Flow Grief.

The morning is bright and fresh outside.

I've already forgotten what I was going to type.

This kind of moment,
a golden podium
for the wise
poets
and not the dead
or dying.

Cold.
I'm not the only one.

For some reason despite being young
I am already strung like a puppet to my past.

My head isn't in this game.

Running nose tells me
I'm not made to last.

Before I know it all my life
will have run out
of me into splatter in tissues
and waste bins

like a river
into the sea.

So why then,
does any of that matter?

Faux.

I don't care for the herd, nor do I want to chase it.
Honestly, I'm disenfranchised with the whole thing.
I hate it.

Or maybe I'm wrong
and I should just wear the
wool suit skin
of old grey wolves
with toothless bites.

Clawing with no grip
on reality.

I am just a man,
wondering among
the wolves
and the sheep.

I don't care for mindless bleating,
or a need to howl my achievements
to a moon that stares
blanky,
tired of wooing.

But it is nice to be in the wild,
and that is a fine
looking moon.

Nuts and Bolts.

I don't know how,

but you dodged the reality check:

You've been screwing and screwing.

If you were suited,

you would be locked

in tight

right now.

Next Friday.

I woke up late in the warm
bath of
a Saturday morning snooze.

Tucked nicely.
Flailing limbs,
soon gasping
when I knew
it was a Friday.

Fuck!
There's no waking from this nightmare.

Time to get up and do it all again.
Toothbrush in hand,
must remember that.
The hair, the hair!

Just one more time,
again, and again.
waiting for the
very last Friday.

Again, and again.

But hey...
This is the last time
it will be
today.

Bumpy Ride.

This is your captain speaking.

We're entering a little turbulence right now,

Rain spits and lashes my eyes,
my thoughts like thunder.
Memories flash like lightning.
The sadness soaked into my bones.

I'm gonna go quiet for a bit,

Everything is fine, don't worry about it.

You might hear some groaning:
This is perfectly natural.

And things might get cloudy.

We're not going be a as high
as we normally
are
after this.

Remain seated.
Make sure your own
mask is fitted
before helping others.

Smoking is definitely,
out of the question.

I grin, like a child on a ride.
Like a game, I know isn't real.
I can't give you odds,
but I've survived every other
time I had this conversation.

Black Sea.

I cannot keep my head above it
or even touch it.

It's everywhere.
I cannot speak,
give up what life is left in my chest.
letting it bubble away.

I cannot reach out.

I cannot see above or beyond what surrounds me.

And I can never hear words of comfort
from any who've been through this.

So, I have no other way.

I don't quite relax,
or let go.

I just lie flat,
at the bottom,
and wait.

My friend silence!
I realise I've missed you!
It's been a while,
 I-
Ah, yes of course...

Succession.

We're fucked.
Total calamity.
Buttons, switches, and red lights,
in my brain's situation room.

We're dead.
Game over, failed.
Only we're not,
so we need to start over.

Total redesign.
New me: what a new idea.
It hasn't worked
the first hundred times.

Who is my successor?
What are they like in professional circumstances?
and fun?

How does he attract the others?

What's the agenda? The goal?
What does this person,
this new person
live for?

Me?

That hasn't worked at all.
I will let go,
let them, be.
See what they get up to.

Nutshell.

It's my dark messenger.
From age fourteen.
Like someone dropped a net over me.

You can't get better
from it any more than someone
drowning can
get rid of the sea.

You learn to swim in it.
And eventually
rise above it.
And realise
you're made of it.

And you learn to dip a little.

But it's only a little while.
Sometimes you need people

to pull you out if it

and that's ok.
Sometimes
the weight
of those people
makes you sink more.

You find your own way.
But it's all ok.
It's all ok.

Knowing Psychology.

I studied the mind
like a prisoner
studies his cell.

Marks his days
and bides his time,
for his final escape.

To know which spots are under guard.

Which parts are being watched.

The new
and the known
passages;
Some, old and lost
forever.

To know the knots of the noose,
the trap doors,
the stage curtain.

Because I'm done
being a thing,
a puppet dancer.

To lose the mind
that assumes all the answers.

I understand the prison,
and some days it's comfortable.

But I have seen too many people
in the same uniforms.

They won't exit the cell
because they believe they were born
in there.

That our brittle lives
begin and end in orange.
and abuse.

I have the courage
to challenge the rules
just a little and not
lose it.

I'm not staying here.
The thing with bars:
You can be drunk at them,
wear them away,
raise them.

What about lowering,
or going under to escape?

A Cold Day in Hell.

I try to break the inertia.
More things are coming.

A man strums with a guitar
and sings
on a bus
at 6:51 in the morning.

There's got to be more
to life
than this.

My mind is low.

The skies grey,
blocking the sun,
blocking my soul,
blocking the fun.

A childish throwaway need.
I can see,

the depression is palpable.

We all wear it over us
like coats and umbrellas
in the rain.

And it'll probably do that too...
Well, fuck it then.

The Shit I saw This Morning.

It's 07:26.
What a wreck.
Bodies, limp, and swaying
with the train carriage.
The man next to me smells like rotten cabbage.

There's so much death in these people.
Extinguished, corpses
somehow still animate.
Technology with scrolling screens
keeps them going without a soul.

I can dip in
and out of this world
just enough
to see the horrors.

And when I really wake up, feeling the world
seep that far into my heart.
I realise the interesting
crazy trip this life is.

I'm glad I can witness it all.
Tell people about it.
The shit I saw this morning.

The Deep.

At the very darkest depths of your mind and soul.
Where the churning waves and stormy skies can't
touch.

No one can see what strobe-light-frightening horror
you've found.

It's too dark in that place.
Most don't have the time to go that far.
You can't bring it to the surface.
It wouldn't survive the pressure.

Even if it did,
it would look
out of this world.
A throat-catching confession
doesn't cut it.

Leave them to their schools
and stormy currents.

Fall into yourself.
Believe in yourself.
Explore.
Drift deeper.
Don't forget to breathe.

I Don't Care About Your Life.

People don't express their souls.

They post pictures of food, their

work, and where they go

on holiday.

As if having an interesting life

is a substitute for a soul.

A picture, a substitute for play.

They try to express themselves by

expressing themselves

in the same way

as everyone else.

Jesus...

Witch Hunt.

I look at the mass grave of my mistakes.

It hangs in the air, but chokes only me.

A grimace on my face.

The closest to sorry my mouth can make.
The responsibility,
I take in full,
down my throat
into the pit of my stomach.

Stone weight to pull me down:

Keeps me from walking
Keeps me from talking.
Drowning.

My trial.
If I manage to stay afloat,
I'll be burned anyway.

I learned;
no one else knows
it's a game.

And you can't lose
if you don't play.

The Edge.

I close my eyes
unclench my jaw.
Release my shoulders
and see this grey world
for what it is.

There's no beauty in store,
though I desperately want to
see it.

Just people,

lost,
torn,
frayed,
and split.

Glassy dead-fish eyes.
Leather jackets,
broken backpacks
and smoke-filled sighs.

It's June, but everyone is

dressed
for rain.
They all know.

I cannot sell myself on Utopia.
A world that wouldn't make anything.
Wouldn't need to shake things up.
Wouldn't challenge ideas.
If the world were even partly, free of sickness,
they wouldn't have built hospitals
for the rest of us.

I'm Gonna' Break.

I'm stressed as fuck.
Constantly working on working,
or taking my personal time
to regenerate
so I don't break
or start working late.

Resting to work?
that's so messed up.
Yoga doesn't work.
The stress is in my blood.

More power,
so I can give it away.

Throw all my energy into a
focused, furious beam.
Piercing into the meaningless void.

If I'm lucky,
I'll be noticed.

But I don't even care about
that.
So what's the point here?

To the Dogs.

Trapped on a train, between crawling
screaming,
babbling children
and two dogs splayed across the floor.

Dogs, heavy-chained like Cerberus,
that might maul
any limb I offer them.

Feed myself to the dogs.

Feed myself to the children,
once they're done
with the husks
of their
20-something
parents.

Feed the kids to the dogs.
The future is fucked enough.

Feed everything to the dogs.
The only wild animals on this train
not making any noise.

Dogs to inherit the earth!
They'd do it better.
I can see the campaign posters.
Black and white, obviously.
Everything to the dogs!

Piglet.

The coach came to a halt
with a gasp as people rose like
meerkats spotting danger.

More gasps, maternal coos.
"A piglet"
I didn't rise from my seat.
It was in the middle of the road.

A woman got out of her car.

A man declared he'd go save it.

The driver didn't speak or move.

Then a predator
driving a cold machine.

And then the spark of hope,
then dismay.

A woman shouts to a five year old
"Theo! cover your eyes, look away!"

Everyone called it a shame.

Everyone thought it was a
travesty.

Crushed under
the wheel of
the circle of
life.
It's flesh and guts
spilt.

No one went to feed on the fresh kill.
No one had the stomach for it.
They called it a shame.

Tomorrow morning, they'll see
the same thing,
and call it bacon.

That's the way it all is.

Rocks.

Both rocks, carried by a river,
clash.

Both rocks think they were swimming.

Both rocks believe they were the victim.

Both rocks know that they intended to hit each
other.

Both rocks feel they are sinless.

Both rocks are cursed.

Both rocks are the hero.

Protecting the best,
and worst of them.

Both rocks are changed forever.

Both rocks are the centre of the universe.

Both rocks are different,

Both rocks were together.

Both rocks are rocks.
Look, we're just pretending. That's all.

Stone.

The bus stops and drops
it's payload and people spill in a flood
of writhing bodies, like maggots
burst from a fresh carcass.

Deliverance
into work.

Cold rain
on my face
like a grindstone.

I can almost feel myself
eroding like statue
complete
with pigeon shit.

Just a stepping stone.
Step by step,
bit by bit.

Towards the last stone
that sticks straight up out
of the ground with our
names on them.

It trips you up
In the end:

You're down.
Game over,
home run.
But for now...

I'm on my way to get my salary.
not paid hourly,
but in reality,
still selling my life,
moment, by moment,
scene by scene
along the milestones.

And I own it
without really knowing
what that means.

Full-grown.

You can see the kids
and you know
the giant teens
will never grow any more.

Which ones will be a success.
The Nobel prize kids.
Which ones will be depressed.
Which fat ones will stay fat.

The ones in phases.
differently dressed.
Already trying to deny
wearing the *jeans*
of their parents.

We know,
because we knew then.

We were told we were naïve to
know the world
by older boys and girls
who believe they've changed
even though,
we know.

Even from that age
our souls were stolen

when we broke away.
The dye packs,
burst from birth.

We are stained.

Carousel.

Just show up, and the work gets done.
Out there, or in here.
It's your scope that's changing.

Fist-sized bulbs, and noise
bright, ignorant, rage against the void of space.

When the night comes you can't
bare to see how small you are.

Bring the festivals.

I can't type anything.
It's all relative.

We can't see what our eyes see.
We can't see your brain, or mine.
The nightclub, the gig...

The carousel goes round.
The great gilded herd knows its way.
They ride rampant, fixed in place and gleaming.
They never touch each other,
not really,

or deviate from place.

Some of the artists and philosophers ride backwards,

or tandem like templar knights.

Their methods are lost to history.

And no matter your choice in steed
they all go round the same way.

And the ride ends.

Ends for the children,
their parents,
and their parents.

The bright lights
stay on.
Shining everything you don't see.

And for a fee, you can ride again.

Different, the same.
You go up and down,
And around.

It doesn't matter.
It's your life.
Impaled by design.

The free animals don't have poles affixed.

You waiver it with your imagination.
Cling to your place for safety.

And if you're a bore,
you don't surrender to the delusion.
Can't stop looking at
everything beyond
spinning past you and away.
You're dizzy with it, which can be
fun, but
you just can't do it anymore.

Back to Factory Settings.

I take five in my bed.

My desires stir my barely
rising
chest and my thoughts.

Agitations march heavy across
my eyelids
with a determination
I can't feel.

My bed is solid,
I don't quite sink into it,
but I'm magnetised here.
Gathering my energy like a
charging pad.

My thoughts are as stagnant
as the
glass of water I drink;
My only salvation.

I'll probably have to restart soon.
But for now, I live like cat.
And cats don't know
about Saturdays.

30 Reasons.

I'm thinking about the balances,
we all do in our lives.

Action, inaction,
Netflix, relaxing.

I'm thinking about my to-do list
that's making its way into the
high 30s.

And I'm thinking about spending
3 solid days
in my bed
with 30 reasons
to get out,
but none of them
good enough.

I realised,
I'm good enough
on my own.

My dreams should aspire
to achieve me.

Silicone.

It doesn't matter much,
so I don't give a fuck.
A touch
lacking sensitivity
in the application of the middle finger.

I've been wrapped in
synthetic
crap
all my life.

The smell of the artificial
still lingers.

What did you
expect of me?
It was wistful thinking.

And I appreciate your mood
minus the attitude,
but when it comes to past wounds
and worrying about the future
I'm all about
kicking
the blues.

I get a new, thicker skin.
I don't bother with sutures.

I don't mind scars.
if it hurt,
I want to remember
because it was worth it.

Loopholes.

You've got to find the loopholes.
Instant noodles,
dark chocolate,
packet of biscuits,
can of red bull.

"silent judgement is deserved, but I'm having a difficult day"

Shopkeeper chuckled, and I found myself smiling.

You've got to find the loopholes.

I slept for 10 hours straight,
and I kept the party going,
being tired all day.

No sentient thought
from the cotton ball
wrapping of my mind.

I was untouchable.
You've got to find the loopholes.

I cleared my schedule.
Suddenly I had time.
Drank vodka with Kahlua,
wrote poetry
and rhymes.

Suddenly nothing mattered.

All the shit
had dropped away.

And that's half of what it is
to be happy.
I can't get the other half,
so I find the loopholes.

Pillows.

The emptiness has a dark comfort to it.

The sleep,

the food,

the drink,

the quiet.

The relinquishing of expectations.

The clear schedule.

That sweet quietness.

Squeezing

yourself for that last drop of

happiness.

Finally, you've got to the point

where you can release.

If only
for those few moments.

Play Dead.

I lay down on my back and expressed death from my
mouth.

My head let the shroud of light descend over my
face.

My body falls away,

I went to the calling beam in the sky.

As I ascended away

from that thing,

lying down, fifty-percent of the time

at least.

My body is no more alive
than the atoms it leased from space.

The minerals of the earth made
animate
with electro-magnetic
energy fields.

So what is this?
This witness;

Who knows this particular show
is to be believed in.
Why him?

Respawning.

I've learned a secret here.

And I never remember this,
until I realise, I've forgot it.

You get to the point,
where your so down
and your body's still going.

Round and round.
Doing this,
planning that.

And you just say

Fuck it.

FUCK ALL OF THIS.

And you just die in your mind.

Lose it all.

Let it all go.

And suddenly,
you got your life back.
And you don't even remember what happened.

Lazy River.

Everyone likes the lazy river.

You remember those
from water parks?

The average man: starts with the
good dingy.

It's pumped up good.

Look at the size of his dingy.

Bigger than everyone else's,
he hopes...

He pumps it more.

He moves fast down the lazy river.

Watch him go.

He's having fun getting
ahead of the losers.

No room for them on
his inflation.

He gets to the end first.

The guy in the yellow shirt
with a whistle says
"it's time to leave now."

"I can't go, didn't you see how well I'm doing?".

The guy says

"Hey.
We all gotta' get off sooner or later".

"Can I take this with me?"

"No man, you gotta' leave it behind for someone else".

Next guy gets in.

It's fun,

but there's a lot of people here;

A lot of struggle.

The current moves in a way that's not his style.

He gets out.

Crazy right?

But not all the way.

He just sits on the edge.
He's still.

Nothing is moving now.

He can just watch things go by.
Mellow.

He stays a long time.

The yellow shirt guy sees him.

"Hey,

you can't stay here forever".

But he doesn't mind.

He's seen enough.

He was ready to get out of the flow,

and chill somewhere better.

Last Guy.

He does nothing.

He just gets in.

And he just lets the river carry him.

He floats on by.

He passes things, people.

Goes this way and that.

He just rides

the whole thing.

See, he knows it

for what it is:

It's a lazy river.

The yellow shirt guy doesn't bother him.

He knows what he's doing.

King of Everything.

The man said he was King of Kings.

The *real* king denied him.

Said it loudly as he could.

He shouted, proudly, riding to every land and wood,
and dusty tavern.

So everyone soon knew
of the "King of Kings".

No choice, the "king" ordered him dead.

But no one would raise a sword,
to silence one man
and his voice.

The king wanted to raise forces.

Destroy the man's homestead.

But no lords
wanted war
against
one man.

The king finally relented
to the man,
who said
not one word.
To the powerful he was resented,
but in
every tavern,
they would sing.

Across the land.
Everyone had heard
of the man,
who was King of Kings.

Underbelly.

The only time the city is united.

is in the dark of night.

The separate parts cannot be seen from a plane.

Above those grey
skies that seem impossible to imagine as anything
else,
is where the truth lies.

The lights come on like veins of fire
bursting from a mangled epicentre.

The cars move along the veins
and you can see the ecology
of human nature
as blood cells.

If you could stick your head outside you would
smell
the breath from its open mouth.

The waste, the street food,
the pollution and cigarettes
that stem from
houses,
designated-areas
and factories.

And you would see that
flirtatious bend
in the pitch serpent that
carves the ground.

The one that invited them all here.
Lynched in that bend
like a noose.

Small boats creep
down it, but many have
forgotten about the secrets
and bodies at the bottom.

All of us tangled and locked into one place
should make us anxious and afraid.

The smog,
and fires
and bombs,
and plagues.

The gravity of this dark matter.

Of this eternal city
that has its day, continuously.

Glasses clink and smash
as we pour gold and red depravity
into its fires
for the warmth
our sins provide.

With each dull bell chime it
feeds on its
dead prey,

wasted on the streets.

Each street linked to the tendrils
to it's great maw.

Drawing in the creatures that
ride its veins.

And we are all of it,
and it's never boring.

KN95.

Fuck
being
happy.

Happiness is like oxygen.
We need it to live,
but if you breathed it pure, you'd be dead in
minutes:
Could you really exist?

When was the last time you checked your oxygen
intake?
Breathe,
like it's not automatic,
or a mistake.

Wake up.
Foil the plans of the nightmare,
or the dream-state.

Spoilers;
it's all the same.

You're making the grey clouds,

and the pink ones.

The wolves
and the sheep
are just
brain-dead people
layered with your thinking.

You breathe.

You feel more alive.

Caught up so
much in your bullshit
its slowly choking
you,
killing you.

It's a noose
around your neck.
A bag over your head,
translucent,
blurring your perspective.

The sun outside loses it's nutrition in the wake
of drills,
of hammers,
of screaming,
dogs, and children.

It's a battlefield;
demons clash in human tanks,
bloated,
pockmarked,

fuelled with ethanol
and vengeance.

They are at war with the world that created them.
I don't want to pretend.

I don't want to sit in my council paradise,
and soak the rays
through engine fumes,
cigarettes,
the smell of burning carcasses
on barbeques.

Remove the covering
of who you think
you are,
because that
is *more* toxic.

You can't filter that
through a mask.

The Butterfly.

I have experienced a great
disconnection.
A butterfly flaps its wings;
Pale white flickers, up and
down rapidly;
Darting and fluttering
between flowers.

No tornados.
But its wings
are so huge
compared to its body.

In one single
twitch

it's up and down.

How can it know what it's doing?
Distracted, or taking it in?
Not sparing one moment
on one single stem,

or flower,
or atom
more than it needs to.

I look at all

the sun warms
in my garden
and I can't see the beauty in it.

I fixate on a dog bark,
or discontent at
dry hands,
that snare me
like a net.
And I'm back in the chrysalis.

The white curtains flourish in the breeze,
animating the cool I long for, in the still heat
of the glass conservatory.

I reach for ice water,
just for a single touch
of the cool surface on my head.

Just enough
relief
to return.

I drink it down.
I take the cold respite internally;
Turning my belly into a cave.

Inside, a serpent
dripping toxic-spite
onto the face of my soul,
between the eyes.

My soul,
chained by arms and legs in the
dark of my rib cage.

In my stasis and isolation.
My winter core staves
the sun on my skin.
Waylays the smiles and grins
I would reciprocate
in the old nation.

The butterfly free falls
like a small paper note.

A memo,
sprung to life again before it hits the grass
and flutters past me.

It reminds me to live.

Sometimes it stops,
and falls lighter
almost than air.

Not sparing one moment
on one single stem,
or flower,
or atom
more than it needs to.

I go back inside.

Cancelling the Games.

After Superman has saved everyone for the
hundredth time.
After spider man has slung every vine-like web for
every mundane...

What I'm saying is,
I'm done
saving you.

Helping,
no.
I'll help until I'm in the grave next to you.

I'll cheer you on the side-lines as you climb the
ladder,
and take a perfect dive,
headfirst into
your
concrete destination.

The X painted
On the floor has worn away
from cracks and blood,
But you're a pro now.

If you want to go again...

I don't understand
but I appreciate it.
But I can't go on
with first-aid packs
of tactical snacks, ice cream-TV-combos
Oreos and emotional flack-jackets
equipped as standard...
Equipped for war.
Equipped as an ally for battle
against your next nightmare.

I can't play anymore.
This is still a game.
It doesn't feel that way when you're losing.
But somehow
I'm bruising on your behalf.

I'm not telling you what to do.
I'm not playing you.
If I was, I might play better.
Who knows.

But if we're going to be dead anyway;
There are more creative
ways to eventually
come home.

So when you are ready
to be silent,
come home.

I'll be waiting,
with ice cream.

Feathered Giving.

I saw coots on my river walk.
Their nest was made of nature's gifts.
Green leaves, reeds and twigs
made an island paradise.

Litter, driftwood and debris made
a fortress with high walls.
They use what they can find
and make do.

Their chicks are red faced with yellow starburst
fuzz on their heads and neck.

They chirp incessantly.
while they are fed;

Parents emerging from the depths;
offerings immediately
in tiny beaks
and forgotten,
too small to see.

They have lost their own marks.
They are bald, with dark tired eyes.
They took turns to paddle
and shepherd
the wayward chicks.

Paired for love, now allies.
They feed them with what they can find.

The world did not end for them.

Corona is not a virus, and still means crown,
the ring light around the sun.

Parents, who gave up their starburst fire.
Lost what made them
pure and beautiful.
Passed the torch, made from their surroundings, that
have changed
since they were born.

Bits of litter instead of reeds for twine.

They can't see the brightness of the sun.
They make do with what they can find,
to feed the blaze
of the little ones.

I see a human daughter
trailing behind,
bored, walking behind a father
with his nose
in a phone.

I see children running past.
Bigger and faster now, but it's not fun anymore.
Going on a run, became doing a run.
That moment, they forget their hearts,

like clouded skies forget the sun.

Sometimes it takes waiting.
Patience.
Saying, "fuck it."
and letting it all go.

And when the reeds sing, and
the river paints, Corona means
the sun in the sky.
Your emerge from grey tones,
and you can see;

You know you are home.

You take in, what you can find.

Cat Drowning in the Shower.

We are all connected,
reconnected,
to an extent
and understood.

Suffering pervades us,
and that connection to it
and to each other
paints fire across the
woods of our hearts.

And when that connection isn't felt,
and they are not
doing their part,

we cross the gap
with hate splashed
like gasoline.

When the inferno starts
going
and the bridge is complete,
we find fire there too.

We hoped if your home burned
you would be spurred on
to do something.

True human beings
are 75% water
and 100% compassion.

It isn't enough
to douse
the whole world.

Next door, a cat screams,
burning and guttural.
Like it is being torn apart,
as it's fires are doused
and given a bath.

I feel anger at the hate and suffering
from these poor
stupid-old-children;
Clinging to the vague
definitions of this game.

Playing like they want to lose.
They need a bath of
meditation bowls
but it is no use,
and not my place
to save them.

I cannot piss on them from my
mounted sermon,

nor pray that they
will find
wisdom.

I must learn
it's not my responsibility,
and that the whole sun we
revolve around
has been incinerating
itself
since the beginning.

We are,
if anything,
it's children.

Some wood,
is for smoke
and fire.

I can't speak for you
but I need to let it go.

I sit in my burned-out field,
with a face anointed
with the ash
of rage-sadness
that I don't bother to wipe away.

Ready to offer a drink
and a break
to any who
wander near.
I have plenty of space now.

Buddha Shape.

The man:

I fucking hate everyone.

But I'm hungry.

I don't think the salve for humanity is found
in mouth pleasure.

I've seen the rotund walking amongst us
without the grace of buddhas.

They got the right shape.

Some are even bald.

I don't think it's from inner peace.

I suspect that is a hairline retreat
across the pate,
from fury and hate,
entrenched in the frown lines to the south.

A butterfly flaps orange
crimson
wings,
like licks of
fire in the air.

We can never be as light,
without care,
or without purpose.

The butterfly:

This is the fucking
worst!

Only a few days
to find a mate,
or be a slave
to death and time,
ready to tear into me
like a panther
in the form of birds,
feet,
or the filthy air.

I broke myself down,

encased in a shell,
my former-self
melted away.

That reincarnation,
for this?

Two minutes to rest
and refuel on a flower,

then back

to flitting back
and forth frantically,

so the ground chasing me from below
doesn't get too close.

Beauty.
All they see is
fucking beauty.

But there's no peace for me.

I'm jealous.

They all look so much,
like Buddhas.

Acknowledgments.

The first and most important person to acknowledge is you the reader. Thank you so much for reading and presumably buying my newest collection. I hope you feel a healthy dose of nihilism and can now happily go about your life having a bit more fun and not giving a fuck. I actually finished writing the first draft a month after publishing Man Made Lemons, and I enjoyed writing this one more, and think it's WAY BETTER.

Thank you, James, for once again vacuuming up my eclectic ramblings about zen, isolation, the liberty of death and, misanthropy, and assembling it into the perfect artwork for my front cover. His Instagram is @Gloomgang and he now has a website where you can buy his art in various forms https://www.gloomgang.com/.

If you liked the book, you can also check out my Instagram @jcambridgepoetry for more poems.

Once again, thanks for reading, and remember

NO FUCKS GIVEN, *Jordan.*